D-DAY

Martha Brack Martin

 Crabtree Publishing Company
www.crabtreebooks.com

Crabtree Publishing Company

www.crabtreebooks.com

Author: Martha Brack Martin

Publishing plan research and development:
Sean Charlebois, Reagan Miller
Crabtree Publishing Company

Photo research: Steve White-Thomson

Editors: Sonya Newland, Kathy Middleton

Proofreader: Crystal Sikkens

Design: Tim Mayer (Mayer Media)

Cover design: Katherine Berti, Ken Wright

Colorization: Samara Parent

Production coordinator and prepress technician: Samara Parent

Print coordinator: Katherine Berti

Produced for Crabtree Publishing by White-Thomson Publishing

Reading levels determined by Publishing Solutions Group.
Content level: R
Readability level: L

Photographs:
Alamy: Pictorial Press Ltd: pp. 34–35; Paris Pierce: p. 37; Corbis: The Mariners' Museum: pp. 3, 24–25; Bettmann: pp. 8, 9, 22–23; Hulton-Deutsch Collection: pp. 18–19; Peter Turnley: pp. 44–45; Getty Images: pp. 4–5, 28–29, 32; AFP: pp. 6–7, 40–41; Time & Life Pictures: pp. 20–21; Popperfoto: pp. 38–39; Library of Congress: p. 14; Photos Normandie: pp. 30–31; Press Association: AP: pp. 16–17; Shutterstock: Bertl123: p. 19; Newton Page: p. 45; Topfoto: The National Archives/Heritage Images: pp. 10–11; U.S. Air Force: p. 20; U.S. Army Signal Corps: pp. 12, 32–33; U.S. Coast Guard: pp. 12–13, 15; U.S. Navy: pp. 42–43; Wikipedia: pp. 30, 40; Army Signal Corps Collection in the U.S. National Archives: front cover; National Archives and Record Administration: pp. 1, 26–27; Raymond Douglas Veydt: p. 36.

Library and Archives Canada Cataloguing in Publication

Martin, Martha, 1967-
    D-Day / Martha Brack Martin.

(Crabtree chrome)
Includes index.
Issued also in electronic formats.
ISBN 978-0-7787-7924-7 (bound).--ISBN 978-0-7787-7933-9 (pbk.)

    1. World War, 1939-1945--Campaigns--France--Normandy--Juvenile literature. I. Title. II. Series: Crabtree chrome

D765.5.N6M37 2012   j940.54'21421   C2012-906748-2

Library of Congress Cataloging-in-Publication Data

Martin, Martha Brack.
  D-Day / Martha Brack Martin.
    p. cm. -- (Crabtree chrome)
  Audience: Grades 7-8.
  Includes index.
  ISBN 978-0-7787-7924-7 (reinforced library binding) -- ISBN 978-0-7787-7933-9 (pbk.) -- ISBN 978-1-4271-7852-7 (electronic pdf) -- ISBN 978-1-4271-7967-8 (electronic html)
  1. World War, 1939-1945--Campaigns--France--Normandy--Juvenile literature. 2. Normandy (France)--History--Juvenile literature. I. Title.

D756.5.N6M32 2012
940.54'21421--dc23
                                              2012040199

Crabtree Publishing Company

www.crabtreebooks.com   1-800-387-7650

Printed in the U.S.A./112012/FA20121012

Published in Canada
Crabtree Publishing
616 Welland Ave.
St. Catharines, ON
L2M 5V6

Published in the United States
Crabtree Publishing
PMB 59051
350 Fifth Avenue, 59th Floor
New York, New York 10118

Published in the United Kingdom
Crabtree Publishing
Maritime House
Basin Road North, Hove
BN41 1WR

Published in Australia
Crabtree Publishing
3 Charles Street
Coburg North
VIC 3058

Contents

Preparing for D-Day   4

D-Day Begins   16

Operation Neptune   22

After D-Day   42

Learning More   46

Glossary   47

Index   48

The Axis Powers

On September 1, 1939, German **troops** invaded
Poland. This was the start of World War II. The war
lasted for six years. Fighting spread throughout the
world. Germany, Japan, and Italy fought on the
same side. They were called the "Axis Powers."
The German leader was Adolf Hitler.

The Allies

Britain, Canada, the United States, and Russia fought against Hitler. These countries were called the Allies. The Allies had many soldiers and weapons, but so did Hitler. The two sides fought fierce battles. They were so evenly matched, no one could tell who would win the war.

◄ *Adolf Hitler salutes his German soldiers as they march into Poland. This invasion started World War II.*

Hitler was the leader of a German political party called the Nazi Party. His followers were called Nazis. The Nazis wanted Germany to be the strongest country in Europe.

troops: groups of soldiers

"Fortress Europe"

Hitler's army invaded many countries in Europe. Hitler called these captured countries "**Fortress** Europe." He thought that if he controlled a lot of countries, he could defeat the Allies.

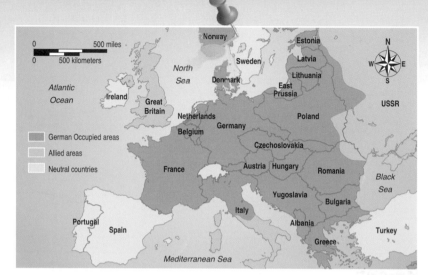

◀ *This map shows Europe in 1944. The dark green areas are countries that were controlled by Germany.*

▲ *These Russian soldiers are fighting the Germans in the city of Stalingrad, in eastern Europe.*

The Allies Push Back

To the east of Germany, the Russians fought hard against the Germans. They stopped Hitler from taking over more land in the east. If the Allies could get into western Europe, they could squeeze Hitler's armies from both sides and take land back.

> Early in the war, the Russian leader Joseph Stalin was on Hitler's side. But in 1941 Hitler invaded Russia, too. After that, Russia changed sides and joined the Allies.

fortress: a strong place that can be defended easily if it is attacked

A Safe Place to Start

The Allies needed many soldiers and weapons to force the Germans out of the areas they had taken over. The Allies also needed a safe place to bring in men and supplies. France was the best choice. From there, the Allies could take back Europe. The only problem was that France was **occupied** by Germany.

▲ Germany took control of France in 1940. These German soldiers are sitting in a café in the French capital, Paris.

▲ *American General Eisenhower (left) discusses plans for*
D-Day with the British leader General Montgomery (right).

Operation Overlord

The Allies came up with a daring plan to enter
France. They called the plan "Operation Overlord."
To begin the attack, the Allies would invade five
beaches in France. They had to get the timing just
right. The Allies would attack by both air and sea
on a chosen day. They called that day "D-Day."

> The "D" in "D-Day" does not
> stand for anything. D-Day is
> army code for the day of an
> attack. June 6, 1944, became the
> most famous "D-Day."

 occupied: when one country has taken control of another country

Spies and Lies

Hitler knew that the Allies
were planning an invasion. He
thought they would invade at the
French town of Calais. It was closest
to England. Hitler sent many German
soldiers to Calais. But the Allies had used
double agents to give Hitler the
wrong information.

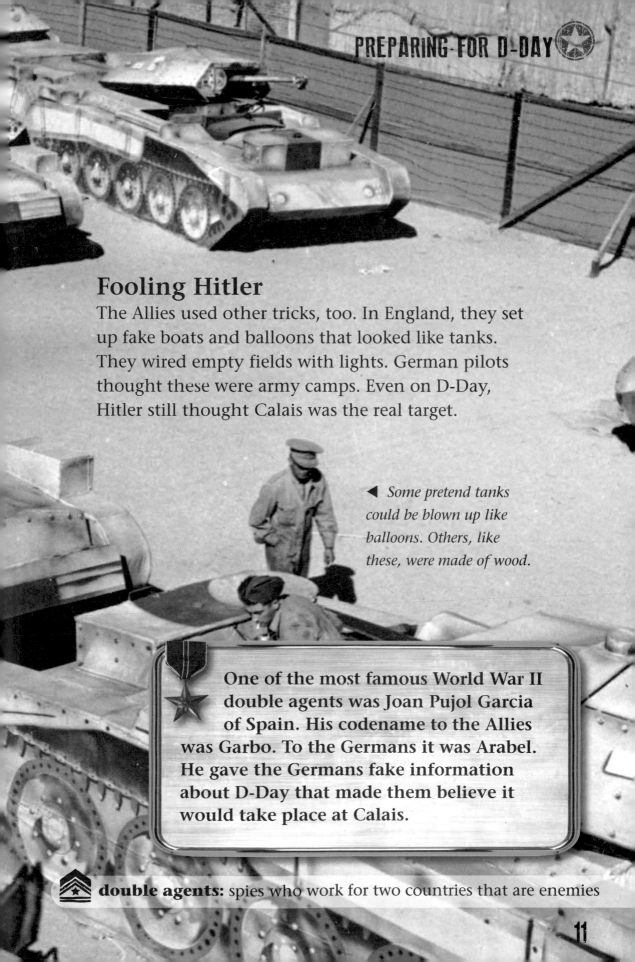

Fooling Hitler

The Allies used other tricks, too. In England, they set up fake boats and balloons that looked like tanks. They wired empty fields with lights. German pilots thought these were army camps. Even on D-Day, Hitler still thought Calais was the real target.

◄ *Some pretend tanks could be blown up like balloons. Others, like these, were made of wood.*

One of the most famous World War II double agents was Joan Pujol Garcia of Spain. His codename to the Allies was Garbo. To the Germans it was Arabel. He gave the Germans fake information about D-Day that made them believe it would take place at Calais.

double agents: spies who work for two countries that are enemies

11

Eisenhower in Control

U.S. General Dwight Eisenhower was in charge of Operation Overlord. He knew the Allies needed more men and weapons for the attack to be successful. Eisenhower brought in another 1.6 million American troops. Thousands of tanks, planes, and weapons were taken to England each month.

◀ *Tanks and guns are loaded onto boats in England in preparation for D-Day.*

Training Missions

The Allied troops trained hard. Soldiers practiced landing on beaches. **Paratroopers** practiced night landings. U.S. and British bomber planes prepared to bomb French roads and train tracks. This would make it hard for German soldiers to get through to stop the attack.

> "We were all eager for action."
>
> Roland Johnson, Royal Canadian Artillery

▼ *These American soldiers are practicing their landing on a beach in England.*

 paratroopers: soldiers who are trained to parachute into battle

May 31, 1944: Time to Go?

About 170,000 soldiers headed to the English coast. They boarded thousands of **landing craft** and bigger ships. This was the first part of Operation Overlord. It would be the largest sea invasion ever. Its codename was "Operation Neptune."

▲ *General Eisenhower wished the soldiers luck before they set off for France.*

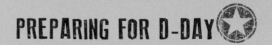
Delay

The men were on the boats, ready to go. They heard that bad storms were coming. Eisenhower held off until June 5. Then he heard the weather would be better for the next 36 hours. D-Day was back on!

> "The free men of the world are marching together to victory."
>
> General Dwight Eisenhower

▼ *Soldiers crowded onto landing craft waiting to cross the Channel for the invasion.*

landing craft: flat-bottomed boats that can land on beaches

15

D-Day Begins

1:00 a.m. to 3:00 a.m., June 6, 1944

About 23,000 British and U.S. paratroopers took off from England. They were the first soldiers to land in France on D-Day. Their job was to capture important bridges and roads in the area. This would stop German **reinforcements** from getting to the beaches.

"Jump!"

As the paratroopers jumped from the planes, Germans on the ground started shooting. Many paratroopers were killed. Others landed miles off course. Some paratroopers landed safely in the right place. They captured the bridges and roads. The invasion from the air was a success.

> "Bullets were criss-crossing the sky. Many troopers were hit before landing."
>
> Joseph Beryl, U.S. Army Parachute Infantry

◀ *Paratroopers had to jump out of the planes carrying everything they would need to fight the Germans.*

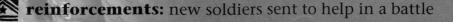
reinforcements: new soldiers sent to help in a battle

Trapped!

U.S. paratroopers Ken Russell and John Steele were in trouble. Their plane had dropped them off target. Their parachutes got stuck on the church in the French town of Sainte-Mère-Église. The Germans could see them. They were trapped.

▲ *The first wave of paratroopers jumped in darkness on D-Day, but more soon followed.*

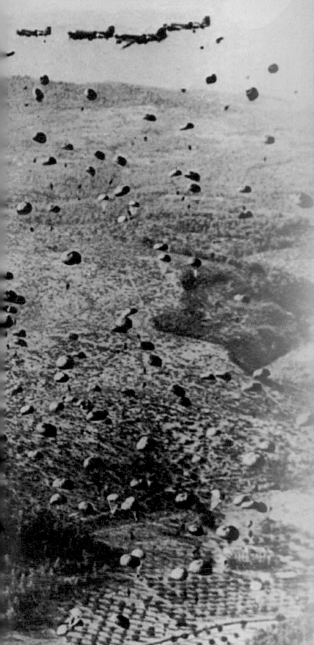

American Hero

Another U.S. paratrooper, John Ray, had landed next to the church. A German soldier shot him. Then the German turned to shoot Russell and Steele. While he lay dying, Ray grabbed his gun. He killed the German before he could shoot again.

> "We were all **sitting ducks** coming down."
>
> Private Ken Russell, U.S. 82nd Airborne Division

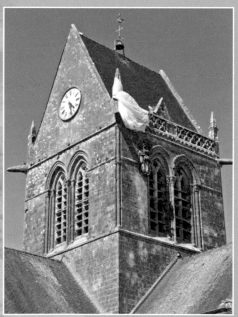

▲ *To honor the brave U.S. paratroopers, a model of a paratrooper hangs from the church in Sainte-Mère-Église.*

 sitting ducks: people who cannot defend themselves

▲ *These bomber planes are on a mission to France in May 1944. On D-Day, bombs were dropped from the air to destroy German guns near the beaches.*

5:20 a.m.: Bombs Away!

Allied bombers flew in next. They needed to bomb German **defenses** on the shore so Allied troops could land safely. The weather was bad. The defenses were hard to see from the air. Many bombs missed their targets. Some planes returned to England without dropping any bombs at all.

5:50 a.m.: Battleships Take Aim!

More bombing came from the sea. Allied battleships in the English Channel fired at the defenses on the shore. They did not hit enough targets. There were still thousands of German soldiers ready to fight back against the Allies.

> "A steady rain was falling and we could hardly see ... But there was no holding back."
>
> Allen W. Stephens, U.S. bomber pilot

▼ *The American battleship* Arkansas *fired big guns at the shore.*

defenses: things used to protect something

Operation Neptune

The Beaches of Normandy

Operation Neptune targeted five beaches for landings in **Normandy**. Each beach had a codename. The U.S. forces landed on "Utah" and "Omaha" to the west. The British had "Gold" in the middle and "Sword" to the east. The Canadians landed on "Juno," between Gold and Sword.

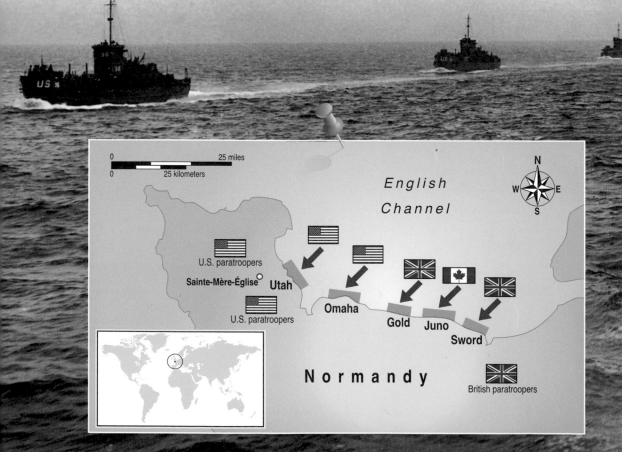

▲ *This map shows the five beaches where the Allies landed on June 6, 1944.*

The Plan

The Allies planned to use landing craft to get close to the shore. Tanks and weapons would be unloaded. Soldiers would wade through the water onto the beaches. These soldiers would try to destroy the German defenses. Then they would move inland to take back France.

▼ *Boats traveled together across the Channel for safety.*

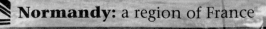

"Your task will not be an easy one."

General Dwight Eisenhower

Normandy: a region of France

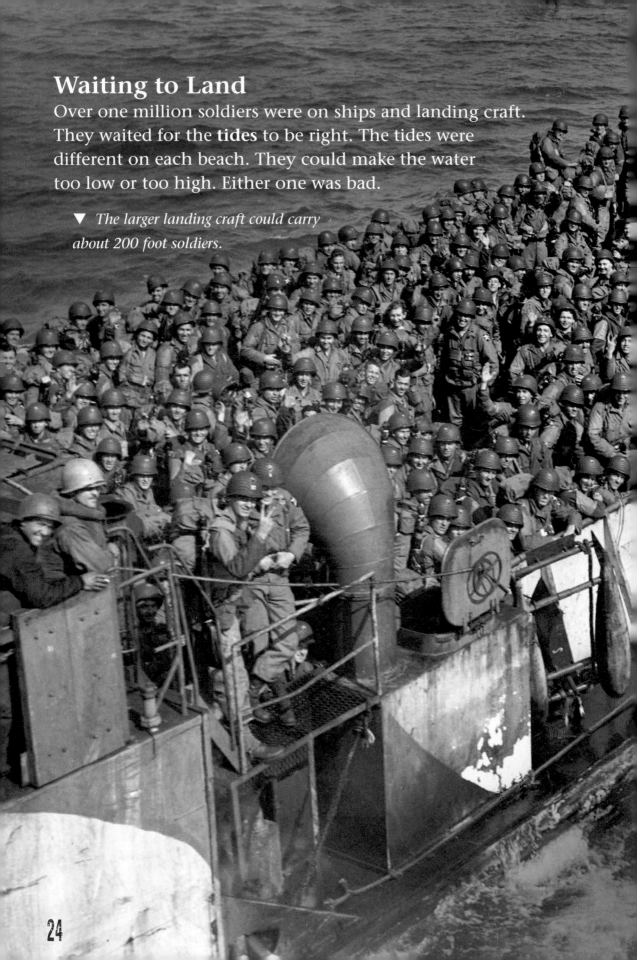

Waiting to Land

Over one million soldiers were on ships and landing craft. They waited for the **tides** to be right. The tides were different on each beach. They could make the water too low or too high. Either one was bad.

▼ *The larger landing craft could carry about 200 foot soldiers.*

6:30 a.m.: Neptune Begins

The Americans landed first
at Omaha and Utah. Then
the British landed on Gold.
The Canadians were next at Juno.
The British forces at Sword were last.
Operation Neptune was on!

The Germans put many "Czech hedgehogs" all along the shoreline. These defenses were made of crossed strips of metal. They destroyed many Allied boats.

 tides: the rise and fall of the ocean

"Bloody Omaha" Beach

Omaha Beach was heavily defended. The Germans put big guns on the high cliffs. They were ready when the U.S. **infantry** soldiers tried to land. Many never made it to shore. A lot of boats sank with their men inside. More than 3,000 American soldiers were killed or wounded at Omaha Beach.

▲ *U.S. soldiers had to wade through the water to the shore, under fire from the Germans.*

Battling On

The men who made it to shore fought hard. They were under constant fire. Slowly, some soldiers made it forward. A few climbed the cliffs in small groups. They destroyed the German guns. By afternoon, Omaha was in Allied hands.

"The bodies of the other guys washed ashore ... my friends ... in many cases, blown to pieces."

Thomas Valence, U.S. 116th Infantry Rifle Sergeant

 infantry: soldiers who fight on foot

Target Cherbourg

Utah Beach was the closest to the **port** of
Cherbourg in France. The Allies needed to capture
Cherbourg so they could bring in supplies after
D-Day. U.S. troops heading to Utah Beach in
landing craft got pushed off course by the tides.
They landed a mile off target.

▼ *Once they made it to shore, the men
on Utah Beach fought their way inland.*

Good Luck

This turned out to be lucky. The place where they actually landed was safer. The Allies lost only 300 men from the 20,000 that landed on Utah Beach. The mission was a success.

> "We'll start the war from here!"
>
> General Theodore Roosevelt Jr., commander of the forces at Utah Beach

port: a place where boats dock to load and unload goods

7:25 a.m.: Landing on Gold Beach

The British came close to Gold Beach, but the strong winds caused the tides to come in quickly. Now the water was too high. They could not see the German **mines** under the water. Many landing craft were damaged by mines.

◄ *British soldiers ran on to Gold Beach under fire from the Germans.*

Winning Gold

British soldiers fought to reach shore.
Germans shot at them from the beach.
Luckily for the British, the biggest German
guns had been destroyed by the bombings
earlier in the day. By the end of the day,
Gold Beach was also in Allied hands.

▼ *The U.S. Coast
Guard helped unload
tanks and other
vehicles during the
attack on Gold Beach.*

Once they had taken Gold
Beach, the Allies built a
"mulberry port." This was
a temporary port so that they
could unload cargo to supply
the troops on the beaches.

 mines: exploding weapons that are hidden in the ground

British Hero

British Sergeant Major Stanley Hollis landed on Gold Beach on D-Day. He was only 23, but he had fought in many battles. Hollis was already a hero to his men. On D-Day he became a hero again.

◀ *A month after D-Day, Hollis was wounded in the leg and sent back to England.*

▲ *These American soldiers have captured a German pillbox like the one that Hollis captured single-handed.*

Stanley Didn't Stop

Stanley's men were under fire on Gold Beach. He saw some German gunners in a **pillbox**. Without any help, Stanley attacked the Germans and took them prisoner. Then he saw another pillbox. He captured the Germans in that one, too!

Stanley Hollis was the only person to win the Victoria Cross on D-Day. This is the highest medal for bravery in Britain.

pillbox: a concrete shelter to protect soldiers when shooting

▶ *Within an hour of landing on Sword Beach, the British had fought their way inland.*

Capturing Sword Beach

Sword was at the end of the five beaches. It was very important to the Allies. They had to capture and keep Sword Beach. If the Allies lost it, the Germans could reach the other beaches and take them back. This would mean that all the Allies' hard work would be undone.

Moving Inland

The Germans did not have very strong defenses at Sword Beach. British troops quickly took control of the beach, and then started moving inland. They were soon stopped by a group of powerful German tanks. This was the only armored **counterattack** that took place on D-Day, and the British won.

"Shells were bursting all around us."

W. H. Jeffries, British No. 6 Commando

 counterattack: when an army attacks to win back lost ground

35

Armored Vehicles

The powerful German tanks near Sword Beach were called Panzers. The Allies knew they had to beat these big machines. They brought their own tanks across the Channel on D-Day. Some Allied tanks were designed especially for this operation.

▲ *Panzers were Germany's biggest and best tanks.*

▲ *AVREs were basic tanks that were adapted to include special features.*

The AVREs

AVRE stands for "Armoured Vehicle Royal Engineers." These were British tanks with some very useful features. They had **armor** at the front and escape hatches on each side. Many AVREs had huge guns called mortars. These saved a lot of lives on D-Day.

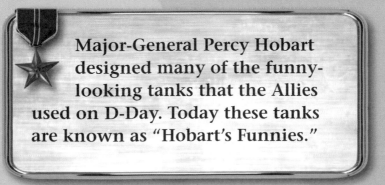

Major-General Percy Hobart designed many of the funny-looking tanks that the Allies used on D-Day. Today these tanks are known as "Hobart's Funnies."

armor: thick metal plates that provide protection

7:55 a.m.: Canadians Take Juno

About 14,000 soldiers from Canada were sent to take Juno Beach. Many of their boats hit mines near the shore. One-third of the landing craft were sunk. Allied tanks were supposed to be on the beach first to protect the soldiers, but the tanks were late.

▼ *The Canadian soldiers were given bicycles so they could carry more and travel faster.*

Never Give Up

The Canadians pushed forward anyway. The men were under constant fire. More than 1,000 soldiers died on Juno Beach. Many more were hurt. **Medics** helped the wounded men. By the afternoon, the Allies controlled Juno Beach.

> "Bodies were everywhere. Wounded. Dead."
>
> Jim Elliott, 22nd Canadian Field Ambulance Unit

 medics: soldiers trained to be doctors on the battlefield

A Canadian Hero

Charlie Martin was a farmer before World War II. During the war he became a Company Sergeant Major. He was a brave soldier. After a battle he went to look for wounded men. He carried them to safety.

▼ The men came charging off the landing craft onto the beach at Juno.

◄ This Canadian soldier is guarding Germans that have been captured on Juno Beach.

First on the Beach

On D-Day, Martin led the first **company** of soldiers to land on Juno Beach. There were 250 men in Martin's company. More than half of them were killed. Martin and two of his men were able to capture a German machine gun. This saved many lives.

> "I was so sad. Fellows I had known for four or five years ... destroyed for nothing."
>
> Charlie Martin

 company: a group of soldiers that train and fight together

After D-Day

The Success of D-Day

The D-Day invasion was a success. The Allies took the beaches, but that was only the start. They used this base to bring in more men and supplies. They kept moving across France. By August 25, Paris, the capital of France, was free.

▼ *The D-Day landings were a huge operation, involving thousands of men and machines.*

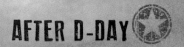

The End of the War

The war in Europe went on for 11 more months. Hitler killed himself on May 1, 1945. On May 7, Germany **surrendered**. Japan kept fighting until September 2, 1945. When Japan surrendered, World War II was finally over.

While the invasion of Normandy was a success, it caused heavy losses on both sides. By the time France was free, more than 200,000 Allies and 300,000 Germans had been killed, wounded, or captured.

surrendered: gave up

D-Day Remembered

D-Day is still remembered today. Every year on June 6, people gather on the beaches of Normandy. More than 60 years later, most of the soldiers who served on D-Day have now died. The few who are still alive are over 80 years old.

▼ *World War II soldiers gather to remember the brave men who fought on the beaches of Normandy in 1944.*

What D-Day Meant

D-Day was a turning point in the war. It gave the Allies a way into Europe. It showed Hitler that he could be beaten. It gave hope to the people in the captured countries that they would be free again.

> "These are the heroes who helped end a war."
>
> U.S. President Ronald Reagan, on the 40th **anniversary** of D-Day

▲ *This memorial statue on a beach at Normandy shows a soldier sheltering his wounded friend.*

anniversary: a celebration of an event that takes place every year

Learning More

Books

D-Day: Day that Changed America
by Shelley Tanaka
(Hyperion Books, 2003)

D-Day: the Allies Strike Back During World War II
by Terry Miller
(Franklin Watts, 2010)

On Juno Beach: Canada's D-Day Heroes
by Hugh Brewster
(Scholastic Books, 2004)

Remember D-Day: the Plan, the Invasion, Survivor Stories
by Ronald Drez (National Geographic Society, 2004)

Websites

www.canadaatwar.ca/content-14/world-war-ii/canadians-on-d-day/
Canada at War: Canadians on D-Day

www.britannica.com/dday
Ecyclopaedia Britannica's guide to Normandy, 1944.

www.veterans.gc.ca/eng/video-gallery?kw=D-Day&fn=&ln=&ct=0&w=0&l=0&c=0&b=0&u=0&o=0&g=0
Veterans Affairs Canada: Canadians remember D-Day

www.army.mil/d-day/index.html
Official homepage of the U.S. Army: D-Day

Glossary

anniversary A celebration of an event that takes place every year

armor Thick metal plates that provide protection

company A group of soldiers that train and fight together

counterattack When an army attacks to win back lost ground

defenses Things used to protect something

double agents Spies who work for two countries that are enemies

fortress A strong place that can be defended easily if it is attacked

infantry Soldiers who fight on foot

landing craft Flat-bottomed boats that can land on beaches

medics Soldiers trained to be doctors on the battlefield

mines Exploding weapons that are hidden in the ground

Normandy a region of France

occupied When one country has taken control of another country

paratroopers Soldiers who are trained to parachute into battle

pillbox A concrete shelter to protect soldiers when shooting

port A place where boats dock to load and unload goods

reinforcements New soldiers sent to help in a battle

sitting ducks People who cannot defend themselves

surrendered Gave up

tides The rise and fall of the ocean

troops Groups of soldiers

Index

Entries in **bold** refer to pictures

Allies, the 5, 6, 7, 8, 9, 10, 11, 12, 13, 20, 21, 23, 27, 28, 29, 31, 34, 36, 37, 39, 42, 43, 45
America 12, 22, 25, 28
Axis Powers 4, 43

battleships **20–21**, 21
boats 15, **22–23**, 25, 26, 38
bombers 13, 20, **20**, 31
Britain 5, 22, 25, 30, 31, 32, 33, 35, 37

Calais 10, 11
Canada 5, 22, 25, 38, 39
Cherbourg 28
Czech hedgehogs 25

defenses 20, 21, 23, 25, 26, 35
double agents 10, 11

Eisenhower, Dwight 9, 12, **14**, 15, 23
England 10, 11, 12, 14, 16, 20
English Channel 21, **22–23**, 36
Europe 6, **6**, 8, 43, 45

France 8, 9, 16, 28, 42

Garcia, Joan Pujol 11
Germany 4, **4–5**, 6, **6–7**, 7, 8, **8**, 10, 11, 17, 18, 19, 21, 25, 26, 31, 33, 34, 35, 43
Gold Beach 22, 25, **30**, 30–31, **30–31**, 32, 33
guns 19, 26, 27, 37, 41

Hitler, Adolf 4, **4–5**, 5, 6, 7, 10, 11, 43, 45
Hobart, Percy 37
Hollis, Stanley **32**, 32–33

Japan 4, 43
Juno Beach 22, 25, 38–39, **38–39**, **40**, **40–41**, 41

landing craft 14, 15, **15**, 23, 24, **24–25**, 28, 30, 38

Martin, Charlie 40–41
medics 39
mines 30, 31, 38
mulberry port 31

Normandy 22, 44

Omaha Beach 22, 25, 26–27, **26–27**

Operation Neptune 14, 22–41
Operation Overlord 9, 12, 14

paratroopers 13, 16, **16–17**, 17, 18, **18–19**, 19
pillbox **32–33**, 33

Ray, John 19
Russell, Ken 18, 19
Russia 5, **6–7**

Sainte-Mère-Église 18, **19**
Stalin, Joseph 7
Steele, John 18, 19
Sword Beach 22, 25, 34–35, **34–35**, 36

tanks **10–11**, 11, 12, **12**, 23, **30–31**, 35, 36, **36**, 37, **37**, 38
tides 24, 25, 28, 30
training **12–13**, 13

Utah Beach 22, 25, 28–29, **28–29**

weapons 5, 8, 12, 23
World War II 4, 11, 40, 43